Apocalyptic Swing

Also by Gabrielle Calvocoressi

The Last Time I Saw Amelia Earhart

APOCALYPTIC SWING

Poems

GABRIELLE CALVOCORESSI

A KAREN & MICHAEL BRAZILLER BOOK
PERSEA BOOKS / NEW YORK

Persea Books, Inc.
853 Broadway
New York, NY 10003

Library of Congress Cataloging-in-Publication Data:

Calvocoressi, Gabrielle.
Apocalyptic swing : poems / Gabrielle Calvocoressi. — 1st ed.
    p. cm.
"A Karen & Michael Braziller book."
ISBN 978-0-89255-353-2 (alk. paper)
        I. Title.

PS3603.A4465A85 2009
811'.6—dc22

                                2009005852

Printed in the U.S.A.
Designed by Bookrest
First edition

for Angeline Shaka

Contents

I

Acknowledgment, 1964

Could have gone west. Could have packed your things,
who cares that you weren't old enough to drive.
Could have sold yourself to truckers
and highwaymen, could have gone down
the dark road between home and somewhere
better, the whole world watching TV and no one thinking of you.
Could've got lost. Could have said, "I don't know"
when the waitress asked, "Where you live at?"
You could have lied and said, "New Jersey."
Or "Mobile." Of course, that assumes
you'd get past Mason Dixon.

You could have seen battlefields:
Gettysburg, Fredericksburg even Chicago
if you waded deep enough into summer. Could have slept
with your head on the ground like your sister,
her ear to the transistor, listening,
listening to "I Want to Hold Your Hand."
You could have said, "Fuck the Beatles"
and left them behind, shooting the lights out
of every stadium, every coliseum.

You could have made girls scream because
you were the stranger under the bleachers, that ember
of the cigarette burning in the darkness just outside their
porch lights' glow. You could have named them:
Helen, Rachelle, Ida May, and in Texas, *Irene Rosenberg*
a girl just as lonely as you. Imagine,

your leaving before it ever got started. *Where's that*
girl you married? You don't know. You were halfway
to Billings or Provo or Bend. You watched the cities
of the Midwest burn. You threw bottles and never
cut your hair. Remember the drum kit in Schlessinger's
Instruments? How you crawled through the broken
window and banged away in the shards of that city.
If they could have seen you then! All muscle
and heart, sweating, sweating, no more stupid melody
holding you back. Just the bass line, just the gas line
hissing and your foot on the pedal.

You could have gotten away. The country was different,
a boy could walk without getting beaten beyond an inch

of his life, without getting lashed to a fence

in God-forsaken Wyoming. Why, God hadn't forsaken

Wyoming or Birmingham yet. Chaney, Goodman,

and Schwerner safe in their beds. Perhaps you passed

by them. You could have passed me by and saved yourself

the whole mess. My mother doesn't know you yet. She's

on her back in the grass with some other man's son.

A Love Supreme

You beautiful, broke-
back horse of my heart. Proud,
debonair, not quite there

in the head. You current
with no river in sight.
Current as confetti

after parades. You
small-town. Italian
ice shop next to brothels

beside the highway.
Sweet and sweaty. You high
as a kite coming

down. You suburban sprawled
on the bed. You dead? Not
nearly. Not yet.

Pantoum Evangel: Billy Sunday

On summer nights we'd listen to him preach,
God loves you and God will cut you down.
Who knew one man could watch over us from
our radio's dark corridors, could hear us

pray for God to love us, to cut our urges down
to a size we could manage. And he played
baseball! Who knew one man could watch over
his glove and see a girl whittled down

to a size he could manage. And he played
till the dark came. I lived in Wethersfield:
was his glove, was his guile whittled down
to the size of a mole's claw. I burrowed

till the dark came. I lived in Wethersfield,
loved the fish monger's son. His zipper near
to the size of a mole's claw. I burrowed
like rats in leeching fields, mouth full of earth.

Near: the fishmonger's son. His zipper: near.
Nearer my God to thee. A song he'd sing
like a frog in a leeching field. Its mouth full
of the spirit. We'd hear it coming through:

Nearer my God to Thee...a song...He'd sing...
We couldn't make out the song's words because
of the spirit. We'd hear our coming through
all of that static and our mothers' prayers.

We couldn't make out the song's words because
of my moaning. I couldn't be quiet
amidst all that static. Our mothers prayed
like crowds at the Beehive, our minor league park.

Of my moaning? I couldn't be quiet
any more than the Red Sox could win one
for the crowds at Beehive Minor League Park.
I can't explain the lure of salvation

anymore than the Red Sox could win one.
I fell to my knees in back of our house.
I can't explain the lure of salvation,
how he shook as I held him in my mouth.

I fell to my knees in the back of our house
as swans came up from our still pond to see
how he shook as I held him in my mouth.
I was like a town on Sunday morning

as swans came up from our still pond to see
the lawns empty but for one on his knees.
I was like a town on Sunday morning.
Was the empty square. Was the parable:

the lawns empty but for one on his knees
and the girl who brought him there, to be watched.
Was the empty square the parable
or were the swans who tensed and chuffed their wings?

And the girl who brought him there to be watched
by anyone who opened their window
or the swans who tensed and chuffed their wings,
where did she think this would leave her but lost?

Anyone who opened their window could
see we looked nothing like rapture. I ask
where did I think this would leave me but lost
as a salesman selling bibles in church.

See, we looked nothing like rapture. I asked
him to be gentle. *He* cried at the end
like a salesman selling bibles in church:
What have I done? I am done for. Please tell

him to be gentle. He cried at the end
and hid himself from me. Billy Sunday asked,
What have you done? You are done for. Please tell
me again how it ended. The swans left

and hid themselves from me. Billy Sunday asked
if I bathed in the blood of the lamb. Show
me again how it ended. The swans hissed.
In the darkness I listened to them preach.

Pleasant Plan Missionary

How to put it on and where to get the bottles.
Schlitz, Old Peculiar, RC. Rummage through the trash
or go to the back of Sumner's store while your brother
stands lookout. Shifty. That's what they say about you
over coffee after church. You'll show them. Some
men are built for nights like this. You've been practicing
longer than they know. Take your fingers,
wrap them 'round the neck, don't worry 'bout
the sweat. It won't take long to get the job done
and you'll be so far out who's gonna see you.
And if somebody did? Well. The mask alone
would scare them back to town. You'll
burn it down alright. Fill her up with so much fire
even Jesus will have to look away.

A Love Supreme

Breathless in the backwoods,
backlit by what joy could hold you,
I see you, naked as stripped wire

all coiled against the quarry man's
hands. You dance the polecat dance,
I lay by the tires, unseen. I crawled

here, sniffing the ground for clues,
bloodhound, girl child rooting you out.
Get gone, you'd say. No way ma mère.

I love you like Elvis loved pistols,
stroking you in the television light,
the possibility of that music

better than all the stages in the world.
Girl, you keep rocking just like so
I'll go down river and catch you a fish

with my dirty hands, no man

can contain the love I have for you

nor the rapt attention. *Take my hand,*

take my whole life too. I've slicked

my hair back, I've made myself

a boy for you.

Dear Elvis, How she did it and when
and what music

Who knows? Not me, sitting in the dark classroom.

Lincoln was president. He was president onscreen.

That's all that mattered to me, a light in dark

rooms, a voice filling the night as I lay awake

and rats scratched in the walls. This was before

I learned to move my hips. When I just lay there

and thought I was dreaming. When the room spun

like roller-rink lights and I prayed you would come.

Elegy Scale

In that black case with
its velvet insides you look
nothing like yourself.

ᛒ

The first time I saw
you, next to the church. He said,
"It's hard for a girl."

ᛒ

Your neck all cork and brass.
The sweet smell of wax
warming as I rubbed.

ᛒ

Sliding the mouth-piece
over. Turning till I couldn't
go any farther.

ᛒ

Who cares if some boy
held you first? This reed slight
and slick in my mouth.

⇝

They called and said,
"We'll kill you." I practiced scales,
the phone kept ringing.

⇝

"Body" doesn't do
your body justice. Patient
in my fumbling hands.

⇝

If all girls had mouths
like yours I'd be done for.

Boxers in the Key of M

As in *Marvelous* and *Macho*, as in Leon's
younger brother Michael, a name I learned

in Catholic school. St. Michael of the mat,
of the left hook and the deafening blow,

of teeth glistening as they made their arc
to the laps of women sitting ringside.

You don't like to see a man get knocked out
cold? Then you've never lived in Hartford

or any town of boarded windows. Have you
ever gotten hit or thrown against a wall?

There's a sweetness to it, that moment when
your God would forgive you anything. One

punch free as yesterday's papers. Marvelous

the way his body moved on the TV

screen. And me? I moved around the room,

bobbed and weaved. I learned to hold my breath

so I could fight with my head held under water.

Every Person in This Town Loves Football

Even the nuns come out
to watch the boys in their
gold and blue. Sister Marita,
Sister Anne, and some weeks

Sister Perpetua who still
uses the ruler on our outstretched
hands. Even the mills
get quiet and how

the new freeway subsides
for awhile so we almost
remember the fields
full of tobacco and feed

corn, the older kids
sent out to harvest alongside
those men who'd come up
from the South. *It's hard*

on the hands my babysitter
told me and showed the small
cuts like netting placed over
the palm. She'd calm me

down when I woke or I'd come
downstairs to find her splayed
out on the couch, head thrown
back and Keith, our quarterback,

working above her. Everybody
loves that sound: all the breath
sucked out of the town and just
as quickly it roars back in,

his arm tensed and stuttering
till he just lets go. From the arm,
from the start of the arc and now
over the heads of Beckett and Pulaski,

over the girls in their short short skirts
to the place where the blast furnace
meets the darkness. Who's your daddy?
If he lived in this town he played

the game too and every girl
held his name in her mouth.
He wore dress shirts on game day
with a tie and his jersey

on top. He walked down the halls
smelling of Old Spice and chew.
Who could break a boy like that?
Who could grind his smallest bones

or show him the bars where men spill
out of their worn letter jackets.
Come Friday we'll turn the lights on.
You'll see us from everywhere.

At Last the New Arriving

Like the horn you played in Catholic school
the city will open its mouth and cry

out. *Don't worry 'bout nothing. Don't mean
no thing.* It will leave you stunned

as a fighter with his eyes swelled shut
who's told he won the whole damn purse.

It will feel better than any floor
that's risen up to meet you. It will rise

like Easter bread, golden and familiar
in your grandmother's hands. She'll come back,

heaven having been too far from home
to hold her. O it will be beautiful.

Every girl will ask you to dance and the boys
won't kill you for it. Shake your head.

Dance until your bones clatter. What a prize
you are. What a lucky sack of stars.

Prayer in the Name of Saint Thomas Hearns

O Tommy Hearns, o blood come down.
Come down on the jaw, from the upper-

cut as the lights cut out on Park Street.
The Ghetto Brothers run beneath the fire

hydrants arc. I love you. Every inch.
And ask that you forget forgiveness

and find your way to Hungerford where my
father glowers over me. Show him

how the bag does penance, how it hobbles
back and forth so rapt. It speeds back to

your cocked fist. It cannot get enough, sings
Sorry, Sorry. Who cares. Amen.

Glass Jaw Sonnet

Glass jaw, chicken neck, bag of bones, heart sick.

Knuckle head, bug eyes, lily-livered chump.

Sweet feet. Heavy handed, gutless, headstrong,

Weak-kneed, barrel-chested, hairless, loose-lipped,

Lion hearted redneck. Hair of the dog.

Brainiac, bow-legged, slack-jawed punk. Head

Strong. Sweet spot. Gut Shot. Back away. Meat hooks.

Lazy eye, on the chin, stink eye, reed thin.

Face only a mother could love. Back down.

Nerves of steel, limp wrist, square jaw. Thin skinned, Soft-

Skull, small of the back, heart strings, limp wrist, green

Eyed monster, cauliflower ear. Knock-kneed,

Slim waisted, eye of the tiger. In God's

Arms. Thick neck. Ass backward. Harden my heart.

Psalm

Who says the grass can't speak?
I hear it clear as water

running in the greenhouse sink.
Hear it hissing in the backyard

of my skull, moving up through
the roof of my mouth till my ears

start to fill with sweet Hosanna:
Halle-, Hallelujah or

　　　　　　　...who knows?
I'll come when called. At night

when the hospital's a mouth
clamped shut or early in

the morning. Who'll keep me still?
Pills and bathtubs filled with ice,

leather straps as worn as

a catcher's mitt, the boy's knees

in my chest. O their white, white pants

starched so sharp I can feel them rising.

Plainsong

There are rooms where nothing happens
and corners where a body can be

left to slump in its flimsy shift
while families take a smoke outside.

There are gardens and a river
and tile as white as clean teeth.

There are fountains and a field.
In the evening after lock-up

the janitors and orderlies play
baseball while the nurses sit and watch,

rocking back and forth clapping hard.

Jerusalem Baptist Church

I have seen the fire from the backdoor of my house.

I have heard the women whisper *Jesus, Oh Sweet Jesus.*

I have counted the cars coming from the darkness of the woods

and have seen the mud splattered on the grille.

I have watched men practice the backhand, the roundhouse,

the lexicon of knots one needs to tie a hog.

I have seen the hog tied over and over as the men laugh

and let it go and call out to know the time it took.

I've heard the men joke hogs are faster.

I've watched them kick one for good measure.

I've watched men wash their hands and put

their gloves away. I've heard *Hosanna* in the street

as the sky grew orange in the distance.

Epistle with a Line from Paul

If, therefore, the whole church assembles
and all speak in tongues saying the names
of the places they've come from—Providence,
Wethersfield, Norwich, Bozrah—who will
first notice the body is missing? Who
will look past the blue iris to the white
wall in wonder. Will anyone ask,
Where has she gone?

              She is not
in the rectory where we gathered
for coffee. She is not in the garage
where raccoons guarded their babies.
There is no place to hold her, no boys
digging a hole. Can you see any breath
rising up from the ground? I lay
down by the river and slept what seemed
like days and when I woke no one
was home.

              Come home I said
from inside my car. I turned

the radio down so I could hear
her if she called to me. It was just trees
scraping the window and plows up ahead
making it safe for all of us travelers.
I drove through fields buried in snow,
the place tobacco grew when I was young.

The Chapel, Now Quite Open to Its God

Nobody home, not yet, each stone just stone

and the ground beneath not yet a town.

Who knows you here? Not a soul. *What name will*

they call you? Rattle-trap, bag girl, girl who

razed our lovely one, placed her mouth on

and let the breath end her for good. *Who will*

lay hands on you? Who laid hands on you? No one.

Nobody, neither preacher nor harlot,

come up from quarries. *What did you want?*

The stable door, merciless against my

back as she lay beside me, on top her

mouth making it well again. *What form should*

it take? Honeycomb, bird's nest, something built

for escape and enclosure. *O Maker,*

who called you, this city lays unmade.

I will build it up again. *With what hands?*

The same ones that held the swollen arms, that

would not let her climb into my bed

and hold me through our mutual longing.

Where will you build it? In the city. No.

On the outskirts of the city beyond

stately houses, beyond the turnpike,

the Big Boy, beyond the graves. I'll build it

in the subdivision of some boy's cowlick,

on the lawn that deepens to blue as ice

hits the evening glass. *Come down pale rider.*

No horse but my worthless, toothpick limbs made

manifest and luminous by headlights

of Buicks purring in the garage. *Where*

are you? I am throwing a ball against

the house as stars come up. I am lying

with my head on her chest. I am dreaming.

What do you see? Her mouth, cavernous as

a horse left to rot in the field, her hair

black as creosote and hot in the nostril

as sex with a cousin. *Breasts?* I couldn't

bear to look. *And what of the harbor?* Just

once, I gazed and gazed and watched it close half-

finished. I begin to let the bloodroot

rot inside. *Will you sing?* O my mouth will

not be contained. I will echo from ranch

house to ranch house, boys will grow hard beneath

their basketball hoops, the girls will lie back
and play the cat's cradle. *Will she come home?*
Never. Not in the side-streets, the bars,
shooting-galleries, she is lost to me
now. I will rock her bones all the same. I
will roll the nails in my mouth and begin
the jagged music.

Epistle From Her Daughter
Yet to Be Consummated Back East

Love, you'll stick your finger into
anything. Sweet cream, valve oil, the mouth

of every damn baby that gargles.
You're insatiable, and that

city will screw you within an inch
of your life. Leave before the sun goes

down, before the cars start cruising
from Sunset to the canyons

and someone writes a song that goes
something like *The city is burning*

as the city startles and burns.
I've got no chance in the face of all

that starlight. Those boys on the beach?
All muscle and grass and nothing

but time. Come back. Pack your cheap bag
and get your ass on that bus.

Prayer After a Long Time Away

God, if you are the horn
and the wind that blows it

then who am I to turn my back
and breath from you.

Too long I say. Too long
since I sat in that cloistered room

beside the cornfield and let
the spirit move me as the Fisher

Price record player strained beneath
the weight of Dexter Gordon

and Jackie McLean. All that vinyl
and the cheap needle that skimmed

along the top as I pursed my lips
and tried to show restraint when

all I wanted was to sound across
the town that bore me so much

ill will. I tell you I'm
ashamed. To have held my breath

so long. To have said, "I give up"
over and over when I could

have made a joyful noise instead.
Were you the songs or the silences

between them, the rustle I took
for nothingness? How young

I was. All those saints
calling to me from the bars,

clamoring in my tin ear.

Rosary Catholic Church

I remember the time she showed it to me, each bead with a carving of a saint inside, chasm between robe and flesh or the hard line of a walking stick no longer than the leg of a staple. That's what faith was, something I couldn't see but felt all over. *Like a charge* she'd say. *Like when they put the wires on my head and I shook and shook.* I couldn't imagine. Most days I didn't even try. Why not play outside or bring every can in the house to the store for recycling? Much better than working the one thought over. Mother in the bed and if I looked closer Mother with the wires, thin as crickets' legs and humming already, before the music even reached. Mother glistening. Mother glowing with the spirit. All the windows of her mind blown out and the light pouring in so you can't tell the fire from the moon. And the organ straining in the heat, the groan of the instrument pushed past comfort toward the highest register. But maybe not, maybe such a low groaning that you could feel it without knowing. How hot the pipes must have gotten. Those men in their white suits stepping back from her body so as not to get caught by the current. *And this is just one day*, she'd say. *This is just one day of suffering.*

Late Twentieth Century in the Form of Litany

The winter continued and I thought I heard voices.
Butchers sharpened their knives and I thought I heard voices.
Roy Orbison moaned and I thought I heard voices.

In the dark room of childhood I thought I heard voices.
My bike chain came loose and I thought I heard voices.
Mother choked on the bit and I thought I heard voices.

A war raged outside and I thought I heard voices.
My saxophone gleamed and I thought I heard voices.
The drive-in went dark and I thought I heard voices.

The speakers kept sizzling and I thought I heard voices.
Boys came in the pews and I thought I heard voices.
Mother choked on the bit and I thought I heard voices.

The mills locked their doors and I thought I heard voices.
Elvis kept playing dead and I thought I heard voices.
I watched her undress and I thought I heard voices.

Boys lit cats on fire and I thought I heard voices.
Flames crept toward our yard and I thought I heard voices.
The Klan marched through town and I thought I heard voices.

I met my maker and I thought I heard voices.

Gas filled the garage and I thought I heard voices.

I lied at confession and said I heard voices.

Someone shot J.R. and I thought I heard voices.

She said, "Get me out" and I thought I heard voices.

My vision got worse and I thought I heard voices.

I crawled into bed and I thought I heard voices.

The highway came through and I thought I heard voices.

I met my maker and I thought I heard voices.

I danced in my bedroom and I thought I heard voices.

The curtains caught fire and I thought I heard voices.

Mother took all the pills and I looked at the clock.

I placed my hand on the turntable and I thought I heard voices.

Joan Jett sang "Crimson and Clover" and I thought I heard voices:

Over and over I thought I heard voices.

II

Training Camp: Deer Lake, PA.

i.

You will head for the mountains.
You leave the girl behind, you say,
"I've got to get my mind clear
and my body right." You pack
a towel, some pajamas and the five
Miles Davis albums your father
bought you all those years ago
when you still played music. You leave
the girl behind with her dark hair
and the dimple on the small of her
back and the cat who never liked you
anyway. What kind of animal
you are or are not remains to be seen.
You get on the road.

ii.

Country is country
wherever you go.
Though you tried to sing
it different for some

time, you know the truth.
There's always a fair
with its attendant
oxen and pies, those

girls cheering on top
of some boy's Ford. When
you drive past so many
places that look like

home and know that you're not
welcome it makes your
heart bloom like the rose
of Sharon.

iii

Sitting in a barn while a man
wraps your hands so you don't break your bones
when you punch him in the face.
That's a privilege.

Mostly you stick to small talk:
the weather, the bear that broke
into the kitchen and ate all the
steaks. Sometimes he makes

it tighter than you like and you
suck your teeth and look at the floor.
He might tell you how to stay safe
in the beating you'll take some weeks

from now. He'll go round the bottom
of the thumb, he'll come down the wrist.
Tender. You'll never speak above
a whisper. He'll leave you to the ring

of your thoughts. How you brought her
honey from the comb, laid it gently
on the counter. How she kissed each
knuckle of your naked hand.

iv.

You start to think about the other guy.
First thing in the morning, zipping up
your jacket as you make your way

out the door. His face, the way he chews.
His hands scarred like yours and all
over her, holding her in the city you called

home. Drinking his coffee with her hand
in his hair, dropping sugar cubes in his cup.
He makes a fool of you, that's what the corner

men say and tell you to keep punching, tell you
to hit him like you've just walked into your
own damn home and he's there using

the hot water, sweating on your sheets.
Don't think of him holding her
while she cries because you'd do anything

to stop the long pull of her sadness.
It's something you can't hit him for.
Imagine him above her instead.

Imagine her teeth on his shoulder,
her voice, how it catches when her neck arches
back just so. And that look of surprise

between the two of you like the end of a record
going round and you letting it go while
you catch your breath? All his now

and forever. The song of you, something
she has almost forgotten the sound of
as you sweat in this godforsaken place

and jump rope and throw the medicine ball
and take a thousand punches in the gut.
Your heart is a field with a thousand gulls

upon it. Let them settle as you work the bag,

as he puts his clothes in your drawers,

as she changes the locks and forwards your mail.

v.

Maybe you don't want to fight anymore,
don't want to sit in some barn
with a bunch of guys who tell you

how great you are all day:
You're a king, you're a lion
in a world of kittens, you're

the toughest motherfucker in Miami,
Detroit, Kansas City. Maybe you want
to slip out while no one's looking

and take the back roads home.
Where's home? Let her tell you.
Maybe you'll call her when you're halfway there,

some truck stop in the shadow of the plastic
plants, young girls making small
talk with guys twice their age. You've

seen it all, gotten hit so hard you
laughed and said, "What's my name?
What's my name." You're the comeback

kid, the cat that ate the canary, your fists
are like blocks of ice in Manitoba
and your arms are the hooks that

swing them. Maybe you'll take
a plane instead, nothing on you
but the clothes you came here with.

Where'd you go? The guys looking
round, *What the fuck?* Oh you're
out for a run, you're out for a swim,

you took a nap by the lake, your head
in the lap of the inn keeper's girl.
What do they know? Once you got

hit so hard you came back to the corner

and puked on the cut man's shoes.

Maybe you're tired of going back in

because some guy tells you to,

you're the Great White Hope,

the Pale Rider, you're the angel

tattooed on your parish priest's back.

Who wants to be an angel anymore?

One time you hit a guy so hard

even he looked impressed before he fell

to the mat and started to seize.

She didn't let you touch her for days

after that. You're a prick. You're a bully.

You're no man she ever wanted to hold.

vi.

For now there's just your trunks and towel,
but one day soon they'll drape you in a robe
of satin and walk you down the aisle
while some song plays that you thought you'd like
to hear before all those bells got ringing.

It's been so long since you've been made fine.
And you love the way it feels to feel
some softness on your back, the sureness
of one perfectly tailored shirt, blue
as the sky in Los Angeles right

before the smog comes in. A surprise.
A girl calling from a distant city.
For now there's just a bar of soap, toothpaste
and a razor. Soon they'll rub you down
with oils until you shine, until you're slick

to the touch. Every muscle has a name
and they'll see every one, that crowd all turned
out in their handmade suits and alligator
shoes. No one will be more beautiful
than you though. Gleaming. Your body burnished

in those lights with the ring girls walking past.
And in the last rounds too with your lip torn
open, your eye already starting to swell. Most
beautiful. When she sees you after
all those months and washes you down, says,

"Easy baby, rest now. Baby, you're home."

vii.

Some nights you walk to the edge
of the woods and listen

for some rough voice to call you
home. And when no one does

you stand a little longer
in the dark, breathing slow

and say your name to the pines,
remind yourself of where

you live, so far from here. Once
you watched a woman walk

down a street you used to know
like the scars on your hand.

It was winter, fire engines
idled as she passed. Who

are you to ask for succor

in the face of so much

beauty. Who are you to ask

this world to remember.

III

L.A. Woman

From this
angle the
girl could
be anyone.
The triangle
of the
city you
see through
her legs
as she
straddles the
lounge chair
where you
lay by
the pool?
Paradise. It's
a canyon,
it's a house
overlooking
a canyon
and beneath
it a

city leading

straight to

the sea.

The girl

is like

a peach

dress on

a dark

night and

who knows

what coils

under the

tires of

some tricked

out Camaro

on Pico

making its

way with

the pills

that you

ordered. You

should think

of the

girl, she's

dancing above

you and

that seems

like something.

Remember the

time you

watched her

for the

stretch of

one block

and then

all night

at some

party on

Sunset and

how she'd

look up

once in

awhile. Remember

how she

held your
gaze? Perhaps
she's a city,
the city
behind her
is just
an extension
of the
swimsuit she's
about to
slip out
of. She's
sweating but
that's just
the heat.
Someone makes
a joke
about Malibu
and you
think the
town but
they mean

the liquor.
She's laughing.
Someone says
something about
a song
written here,
maybe The
Doors or
Hendrix anyway
someone was
really high
and someone
almost got
shot. Keep
your eye
on the
girl. She
wasn't born
here but
she's doing
just fine.
You don't

have to

talk about

Keats. You

don't have

to prove

one damn

thing. Don't

have to

spend the

whole day

with a

bullet in

your mouth.

Lie back.

Interrogate the

slow jam.

Find the

space in

the hollow

of her

collarbone that

will make

her fuck

up the

lyrics when

you place

your lips

there. The

objective correlative

of her

collarbone. She's

read lots

of poems.

She'll think

it's funny.

She's not

from around

here. You're

doing just

fine.

Fence

They took that boy and tied him to a fence
and beat him till he didn't know his mother's
name.

They walked into a bar and saw a boy and
said they'd drive him home.

They saw a boy who sat beside the radio
singing *O L'Amour* and imagined one sure
tongue moving down his body in the middle
of the dance floor in a golden city.

They took that boy and tied him to a fence
and proved a brain can seep and freeze
outside the skull.

They walked into a bar and saw a boy and
asked him for three dollars and beer.

They saw a boy who held himself as the song
played and have you ever thought you would
give anything to get out of the four walls
of your life?

They took that boy and tied him to a fence
and beat him till he broke and left him there
in the cold.

The Halfway Girl

In the empty house I listen to him sing.
Awash in the light of the living-

room I turn him on, Live in Las Vegas
but so close I can climb inside that vinyl

and shake and make the girls moan and pull
their hair. I'm onstage and there's just one

girl out there, just one in the crowd. She's come
all the way to see me. She's hitched and saved up

her welfare checks. Maybe she's worked extra
hours all week and in between songs we breathe

and wait out the silence until it starts
all over again like suburbia's lights:

first one then the whole street ablaze and no
one's drawn the curtains yet so you can see

everybody and they can hear me.

Box Fugue

For here there is no television
that does not see you, no suburb

whose garage doors do not open
as men stroll out to speak

about the blows you took. You
are like so many Buicks on the

conveyer belts of Flint, splendid
and silenced. Who knows Duk-Koo Kim

in Wethersfield or Allentown or any
town but Seoul? You are like the rains

in Las Vegas: fleeting, a memory
before the man can even think

to stop it. I saw you once against
the ropes. I heard a man say your name

as a joke. Duk your mother
is a suburb of a fist, her mouth

takes in the gun. All our mothers
have to die one day. I think I knew that

even then. Your trunks were golden
and the palm trees shook at Caesars

Palace. We are all so beautiful
with our face against the mat.

Jubilee

Come down to the water. Bring your snare drum,
your hubcaps, the trash can lid. Bring every
joyful noise you've held at bay so long.
The fish have risen to the surface this early
morning: flounder, shrimp, and every blue crab
this side of Mobile. Bottom feeders? Please.
They shine like your Grandpa Les' Cadillac,
the one you rode in, slow so all the girls
could see. They called to you like katydids.
And the springs in that car sounded like tubas
as you moved up and down. Make a soulful sound
unto the leather and the wheel, praise the man
who had the good sense to build a front seat
like a bed, who knew you'd never buy a car
that big if you only meant to drive it.

Praying With Pat

Come to think of it I was running
already, though not from them.
I was just stretching my legs, feeling
the new road out. A bridge got built
when the highway came through and all
those fields got paved over.

No it wasn't a tragedy, just more
noise and one less place for me
to hide. Nowhere hides you better
than a wheat field. The wind makes
a cymbal from the chaff so all
you hear is the steady *chhhhhh-chhhh*
not so different from traffic

just a higher pitch and more
modulation. Right, like the difference
between someone who's been playing
a long time and a kid in seventh
grade band. So I was feeling it
out and it wasn't bad pounding
above all of that progress. We'd never

had *progress* before. I was proud
of my body and how strong it felt.
It hadn't always been that way
but that's another story. Funny,
as I tell this I can hear them
coming. I'd like to warn myself.
Of course now I listen. I know

how a truck sounds as it slows down
just enough to get the job done:
imagine rolling all the field
drums into the closet at the end
of band practice and you've just about
got it. You can feel it in your gut
like Monday coming. I was so close

to home that almost no one saw me
soaked in spit and Cola, a deep blush
forming where the bottle hit my thighs.
I have been meaning to write you
for some time but it was surprising
how hard it was to speak of this
thing we have in common.

Blues for Ruby Goldstein

The best time is sunset when the streets get

quiet. No more kids playing stickball

under the window. No guys looking up

to see if you're home. What does anybody

know about a body anyway?

It can take a worse beating than most

can imagine. You can get every rib broken

and your eyes punched shut and your kidneys

can bleed like you see at the butcher. You can

forget your name and still be in church

the next morning passing the plate. It's why

guys like to get in fights at the bar:

no one who's taken a punch really thinks

he'll get killed. I mean sometimes it's different.

One time out on the street this kid mouthed

off to a cop. Just some skinny kid not from

around here, probably he lived further
uptown. They took him round the back
of my building and let him know what was what,
how this part of town ran. I remember

him down on his knees, not making a sound
just slumping forward and rocking back
as he took the boot in the face. One would
grab his head like a barber checking the length

of his hair. And he'd pull so the kid rose up
a little and then he'd let go. It went on
like that for awhile. That kid probably
thought he was done for. Yeah. He probably

thought they'd leave him for dead. Which they did.
He was slight. What we'd have called a flit
or a fairy. Or something unkind. But you know?
He got up a few hours later. At first

he just crawled but he found his legs
pretty soon. He got up and looked around.
You could see him take a big breath before
he walked into the street. That was brave

for that kid to do that. And the guys let him
go without making much of a fuss. I think
a beer can got thrown and maybe a couple
guys spit. Nothing too bad after what he'd

been through. I was skinny myself. "The Jewel
of the Ghetto." That's what they called me back
in the 30's. So I know the kind of
lip you take from guys bigger than you.

All heart. That's what most little guys are.
But that counts for a lot. In the gym or
the ring all you gotta do is get up
one more time than the other guy thinks you can.

It's true. Nothing breaks a guy's spirit
like a skinny kid getting up off the floor.
Some nights I could see the moment I won
before I won. I'd take every punch

that some fighter could think of, I'd feel them
just let themselves loose in my gut till they
let go, or sometimes the gut and the head
and the gut one more time and here's something

no fighter will tell you: there's a sound
you make when you hit and you hit and you're
nothing but motion. It's not like sounds
you make with your wife or a girl, it's rougher

and darker and sometimes it feels better
and after you feel so relaxed. You can't
really explain it and make it sound
normal. But a lot of folks know what I

mean. And I'd let the guy do it, let him
get to where he'd want me to hold him
up for a bit. He would almost thank me
for not falling down. We'd stand there till

the ref pushed us apart. Both of us catching
our breath. And those big guys just couldn't
believe it, that I was still there, not passed
out on the mat. One time I even whispered,

"It's over" in this guy's ear. Real quiet
so as not to embarrass him. Just, "Look."
And then I walked back to my corner
and then I came out and punched him once

in the jaw. He looked up like someone called
him for dinner and then he just fell.
I can still see him against the blue of the mat
like when you're lying down and a man

comes into view above you with the whole sky
behind him.

What I'm trying to say is
a body can take a hell of a lot. It's
100 degrees today in this city.
And still the kids are out on the streets,

the women are outside at the market,
there's the girl in the next building learning
to play violin. And sure they're all sweating
and wiping their foreheads but who's gonna

say, "Stop." They don't want to. That's the truth.

Temple Beth Israel

I thought I would write to you about the bombings
Of all those churches and temples in the South.

But instead I took a corner and there
Like the sun I wake to in this distant city

A boy resplendent in his yarmulke and Lakers
Jacket. It has happened before but we are almost

Champions now. In the arena, on the radio,
On every school bus there is the song of our city

Winning something. He was no higher than
My chest, heaving from a run as I tried to burn

Off a night of restless dreams. I thought
I would write about the people standing on the corners

In the midst of all that rubble and destruction
But here are the fathers carrying their sons to shul

And my legs are moving like I always dreamt they could.
If I could talk to you amidst all this traffic and choose

To speak of joy instead of the suffering of so many—
People laughing in the streets: Shenandoah, La Cienega,

Doheny with its schools and girls in their long skirts—
does this make this less of a poem? How do we make a world

When so many don't want us here? Here are the boys
In their black suits and golden jackets. Here are the hills

Dry from months with no rain. Here I am learning
To read again. We sound the alarm and it is as sweet

As it is sorrowful. Our hands are in the air. We are running.
We are using our legs. We are holding buckets of water

And bright flags. We wear jerseys with the names of temporary
kings upon them. We are breathing. We are breathing.

We are almost champions now.

Notes

"Acknowledgment, 1964" is for Thomas Calvocoressi.

Pleasant Plan Missionary Baptist Church was one of numerous churches bombed by members of the Klu Klux Klan. Jerusalem Baptist Church was bombed by members of the Klu Klux Klan in 1964. Rosary Catholic Church was also bombed by members of the Klu Klux Klan in 1964.

"Epistle with a line from Paul" references 1 Corinthians 14:23.

"Epistle From Her Daughter Yet to Be Consummated Back East" takes its first line from Robert Altman: "Wisdom and love have nothing to do with each other. Wisdom is staying alive, survival. You're wise if you don't stick your finger in the light plug. Love—you'll stick your finger in anything."

"Late Twentieth Century in the Form of Litany" is written after Tom Andrews' poem "In the Twentieth Century."

"Box Fugue": Duk-Koo Kim (January 8, 1959 - November 17, 1982) was a South Korean lightweight boxer who died after a boxing match with Ray "Boom Boom" Mancini.

"Jubilee" is for Nelson Eubanks.

"Praying with Pat" is for Pat Rosal and owes an enormous debt to his book, *My American Kundiman.*

"Blues for Ruby Goldstein": Ruby Goldstein, also known as "The Jewel of the Ghetto" was a welterweight who fought from 1925-1937. He was five feet, four-and-a-half inches, and had a record of 50-5. Goldstein may be best known as the referee in the Emile Griffith-Benny Paret title match on March 24, 1962. Paret was knocked out in 12 rounds and died on April 3rd from injuries while trapped, helpless, on the ropes. Goldstein was criticized for not stopping the fight earlier, though a New York Commission hearing cleared him of any wrong-doing.

"Temple Beth Israel" is for Alicia Jo Rabins. The synagogue was bombed in September 1967.

Acknowledgments

Grateful acknowledgment is given to the following journals where these poems appeared:

Columbia: A Journal of Literature and Art: "A Love Supreme,"
   "The Chapel Now Quite Open to Its God."
Guernica: "Acknowledgment, 1964."
Gulf Coast: "A Love Supreme," "Prayer in the Name of
   Saint Thomas Hearns."
New England Review: "Boxers in the Key of M," "Epistle From
   Her Daughter Yet to Be Consummated Back East."
Quarterly West: "Jubilee", "Prayer After a Long Time."
Sou'wester: "Box Fugue", "L.A. Woman."

"A Love Supreme" also appeared in *The Music Lover's Poetry Anthology* (Persea Books, 2007) and on *From the Fishouse* (www.fishousepoems. org) and will appear in *The Everyman's Library Book of Horse Poems*.

"Acknowledgment, 1964" also appeared on *From the Fishouse* (www.fishousepoems.org).

This book was made possible by support provided by a Jones Lectureship in Poetry at Stanford University.

The completion of this book would not have been possible without the help and support of family and friends. Special thanks goes to Thomas Calvocoressi, Ameya Calvocoressi, Lisa Calvocoressi, Gertrude Martin, Frances Offenhauser, Michael Mekeel, Mikie Mekeel, Paige North, Jennifer Lind, Alexis Raben, Miguel Sapochnik, Erin Zimring, Daniel Pipski, Damon Van Deuson, Molly Smith, Wendy Spero, Amos Elliston, Yoshi Shaka, Helina Shaka.

For fellowship, inspiration, and support, thanks goes to C. Dale Young, Ellen Bryant Voigt, Peter Turchi and the entire Warren Wilson community, Jennifer Chang, Aaron Baker, Robin Ekiss, Pat Rosal, David Adjmi, A. Van Jordan, Matt O'Donnell, Brian Teare, and Lytton Smith.

Thanks to Michael Braziller and Karen Braziller, to Dinah Fried, and to all of the Persea interns at the University of Missouri.

Thanks to Kim Witherspoon and Inkwell Management.

Nelson Eubanks, Julie Orringer, Sean Singer, and Alicia Jo Rabins. Abiding.

For Gabriel Fried: editor, champion, and friend.